Milestones
in Icelandic History

Iceland
Review

Text © Jón Ólafur Ísberg 1996
Illustrations © Brian Pilkington 1996
English translation: Gary Gunning
Design: Erlingur Páll Ingvarsson
Published by Iceland Review, Reykjavík, Iceland 1996

Printed in Singapore

ISBN 9979-51-103-6

Foreword

The Viking Age (8th-11th centuries) witnessed a massive expansionary movement of the Nordic peoples across Europe.

Wherever the Vikings settled however, they had to contend with already existing populations, a situation leaving only two possible outcomes: to purchase land or take it by force and subjugate the natives.

History abounds with tales of Viking cruelty, but in reality excesses were not directed against general populations, who were usually unprofitable targets anyway, but rather against the laity and the learned upper elements of society.

It is also a misconception to label all Vikings as

warlike. The Vikings also numbered among their ranks merchants, traders, farmers and craftsmen, all of whom were eager to found a new future away from their overcrowded homelands. In the 9th century Vikings came across an uninhabited island in the North Atlantic which they named Iceland. As news of the discovery spread, settlers from Viking regions around north and west Europe flooded into the new country, bringing with them families and whatever goods they could fit into their longboats. From these roots Iceland quickly developed a unique culture moulded both by the island's physical environment and the settlers' origins, and it is the only European nation that knows its story from the beginning.

870 930 The Age of Settlement

THE TITLE OF ICELAND'S "first official resident" goes to the Norwegian settler Ingólfur Arnarson, and it is customary to say that 874 is the year when he started his settlement. Following Viking practice, Arnarson cast his high-seat pillars into the waters off Iceland and vowed to settle wherever they were washed ashore.

The pillars came to land in a bay he named Reykjavík, and it is a peculiar coincidence that later this bay became the site of the capital city of Iceland.

The optimistic Arnarson was soon followed by about 430 settlers and their families, mentioned in *Landnámabók* (the Book of Settlement), and all available farmland was claimed within sixty years.

 ## 930 Founding of the Althing

INTENDING TO MAINTAIN their new-found independence, Iceland's new inhabitants lost no time in organizing a parliament which they called the Althing. The new assembly was founded on the Thingvellir plains in the southwest of Iceland.

The Althing was under the direction of 36 "godar," prominent chieftain priests who held both judicial and legislative powers, with the ultimate source of executive power residing among the people. With time however, a lack of common aims among the powers led to the gradual emasculation of this noble attempt at self-government.

 ## 985 / 1000 The Discovery of Greenland and America

EIRÍKUR THE RED, a brawny seafarer, is cred-

ited with stumbling across a huge tract of
frozen land to the west of Iceland. Blessed
with a sense of irony and eager to attract settlers to the new Eden, Eiríkur gave his discovery the enticing name of "Greenland"
and during the next few years a steady stream
of Icelanders moved over there.

Eiríkur's son, Leifur the Lucky, discovered
the North American mainland, about fifteen
years later, and possessing his father's way
with words, named it "Wineland." Icelandic
settlements continued in Greenland until
the 15th century before disappearing into the
mists of history.

1000 Christianity Comes to Iceland

SEVERAL OF THE ORIGINAL settlers were
Christians, but the majority were unconverted
heathens who still worshipped Thór and Ódin
and believed in Valhalla.

Following much heated debate, it was decided
at the Althing to adopt Christianity for the entire country, as the legislators felt that one law
and one faith were the bases for the peaceful
development of the country. Tolerance was,
however, the key note of the general conver-
sion to Christianity, with heathen practices
which were not too blatant mostly ignored.

1056 The First Bishop

ÍSLEIFUR GISSURARSON was consecrated as Iceland's first bishop by the Archbishop of
Bremen. Fifty years later Iceland was divided
into two main areas of Church administration
with the creation of one diocese for the north
of the country and one for the south. Until
1800 the bishops were based at Hólar in Hjalta-
dalur valley and at the major ecclesiastical centre of Skálholt, when both episcopal sees were
combined and moved to Reykjavík.

 1104

Hekla Eruption

THIS FIRST RECORDED ERUPTION of Iceland's
star volcano triggered immense devastation
and caused lasting desolation to entire swaths
of neighbouring countryside.

Since its debut in historical times, Hekla has
kept up a hectic career, erupting no fewer
than 20 times between 1104 and 1991.

A spectacular display of geothermal power by
Hekla in 1947 is still considered to be one of
the greatest eruptions anywhere on earth this
century.

Hekla has long been a favourite with volcano enthusiasts, and its angrily smoking crater was thought by bygone "scholars" to be the entrance way to hell!

 ## 1130 Beginnings of Recorded History

A PRIEST BY THE NAME of Ari the Learned wrote the first outline of Icelandic history, starting from the beginning of the settlements up until his own times. His work is known as *Íslendingabók* (the Book of Icelanders) and he wrote it in the vernacular which was a very wise thing to do as never before had a book been written in Icelandic. Apart from its linguistic significance, the "Book of Icelanders" has provided researchers and scholars with an invaluable fund of knowledge on early Iceland.

 ## 1133 First Monastery

DESPITE ITS RELATIVE geographical isolation, Iceland was not immune from the wave of monasticism that swept medieval Europe, and Iceland's first cloister of Benedictines

was established at Thingeyrar, north Iceland. In time the number of monasteries grew to seven, while two convents were also founded. These religious establishments were to remain Iceland's main centres of learning and culture throughout the medieval period.

The monasteries survived until the mid-16th century when, with the coming of the Reformation, they were abolished.

1178 Birth of Snorri Sturluson

THE GREATEST AND MOST FAMOUS Icelandic

author and historian of the Middle Ages, Snorri Sturluson, was born in 1178.

He was brought up at the estate of Oddi, south Iceland, where he got a very solid preparation for the future and an excellent education. Later Snorri went on to write such major works of medieval European literature as *Heimskringla*, the *Edda* and possibly *Egil's Saga*.

Snorri was also a keen power broker in the often treacherous political life of his time, but he was perhaps better acquainted with manuscripts than broadswords, for he was murdered in 1241 at his home in Reykholt, west Iceland.

 1262 The End of Independence

FOLLOWING THE DECADES of civil strife that have come to be called the "Age of the Sturlungs," in turn identified with the then political elite of Snorri Sturluson's family and followers, Iceland's chieftains decided to submit to Norwegian overlordship.

Peace has been a permanent fixture ever since, no doubt partly explained by the fact that Icelanders have never had an army.

Following the union of the Danish and Norwegian crowns in 1380, Iceland became
subject to Danish rule, a position that was
not finally changed until 1944.

1362 Natural Catastrophe

A TREMENDOUS ERUPTION just south of Iceland's largest glacier Vatnajökull, which also
happens to be the largest glacier in Europe,
caused immense loss of life and left the sur-
rounding areas a wasteland for the next several centuries.

Following this catastrophe, the glacial site of the eruption was named Öræfajökull or "Desolation Glacier." The ominously titled mass of compact ice is the setting for Iceland's highest peak, Hvannadalshnjúkur, which towers a majestic 2,119 metres above sea level.

The Coming of the Plague

AFTER RAVAGING MAINLAND Europe for decades, the plague finally struck Iceland, where it swiftly killed about 30,000 people which was almost half the population. Recurrent outbreaks, plus the arrival of smallpox and intermittent famine, kept population levels low for the next four centuries. The paucity of inhabitants meant that childhood diseases originating from Europe soon acquired epidemic proportions in Iceland, although geographical distance did go some way toward limiting the frequency of outbreaks.

The First Fish War

HIGH FISH PRICES in Europe soon attracted

English and German merchants to Iceland's
rich fishing grounds, where competition
quickly gave way to confrontation.
Eventually an alliance between German
Hanseatic League merchants and the Danish
King succeeded in dislodging the English,
but not before the English had achieved a
considerable level of influence in Iceland's
affairs.
Before their departure the English had even
brought the episcopal sees under their sway
and had gone so far as to kill the Danish
King's Governor in Iceland.

1540 / 1550 The Reformation

FOLLOWING THE RELIGIOUS wars and the adoption of Protestantism in Denmark in the period 1533-36, Lutheranism was imposed upon Iceland, and the country's first Lutheran bishop was consecrated at the renowned ecclesiastical centre of Skálholt in 1540. Iceland's other major church centre at Hólar remained under the control of Jón Arason, Iceland's, and Scandinavia's, sole surviving Catholic bishop.

Arason and his two sons were eventually beheaded at Skálholt in 1550.

1584 Gudbrandur's Bible

THE FIRST ICELANDIC-LANGUAGE book to be printed in Iceland was a translation of the Bible which emerged from the presses at Hólar.

The driving force behind this benchmark in Iceland's long literary culture was Bishop Gudbrandur Thorláksson, a learned scholar who not only translated the text but also helped make the actual printing blocks. Thorláksson's Bible translation was subse-

quently to have a decisive influence on the future development of the Icelandic language.

 ## Trade Monopoly

THE DANISH KING sold merchants from Denmark exclusive licences to trade with Icelanders and with Icelandic produce. Such a trade monopoly of course guaranteed substantial incomes for the ruling powers, but it also proved to be a major obstacle to economic development in Iceland. The Danes' monopoly on Icelandic trade was removed in 1787.

Renaissance High Point

THE HISTORY OF ICELAND, *Crymogæa*, was written in Latin by Arngrímur Jónsson, one of Iceland's foremost representatives of Renaissance scholarship.

His publication aroused the interest of fellow scholars in early Icelandic historical research across the length and breadth of Europe.

To this day, the appearance of Jónsson's book is regarded as a groundbreaking event that laid the foundations for further serious investigation of Iceland's history.

 Absolute Monarchy

ICELAND'S MOST INFLUENTIAL men agreed to submit to the personal absolute monarchy of the Danish King, in return for recognition of their privileged position. Despite this development in Icelandic-Danish relations, Icelanders were, for the most part, left free to govern their own affairs. In addition to being exempt from military service, Icelanders were not forced to contribute higher taxes to the Danish treasury. Nor were Icelanders compelled to adjust to any new laws arising from the shift to monarchy.

1666 Hymns of the Passion

NONE TOO SURPRISINGLY it was a priest,
Hallgrímur Pétursson, who wrote the most
famous pieces of devotional literature to
have emerged from Iceland.

Pétursson's series of hymns deals with the
passion and crucifixion of Christ. It has been
recognized as a classic of Icelandic writing
and translated to several languages.

Today the towering spire of Hallgrímskirkja
church dominates the capital's skyline in his
memory.

Final "Witch" Burning

THE LAST BURNING of a man accused of practising the black arts took place sixty years after the first unfortunate "witch" met a similarly heated fate. In striking contrast to the norm on the European mainland and in Puritan New England, most of the Icelandic victims of the witch craze were men. Most of the twenty-three men and two women who died at these grisly executions were from the West Fjords of Iceland, which were understandably thought to be haunted for a long time afterwards.

The First Census

THE FIRST CENSUS of the population of an entire country was carried out in Iceland, and the results of the count showed 50,358 inhabitants to 8,191 dwelling structures.

In the southwest corner of Iceland, where over fifty percent of the present population lives, the 1703 census showed only eight percent in residence. Iceland is the only European nation that can claim to have kept continuous records of settlement dating back to the country's discovery.

1707 1709

Fresh Epidemics

As most European countries were experiencing population explosions, Iceland was once more stricken by the return of smallpox. Not only was the epidemic a severe blow to the country's economic development, the outbreak of the disease killed or led to the death of about 18,000 people, about one third of Iceland's inhabitants. The tragedies of the early 1700s were to set the tone for the rest of the century, and Iceland's population was to remain at precariously low levels for decades to come.

The Enlightenment

THE GREAT INTELLECTUAL ferment known as the Enlightenment made a belated but none the less influential appearance in Iceland during the late eighteenth century.

Despite much opposition and resistance, new channels of communication were opened between Iceland and Denmark, and many prominent Icelanders played a leading role in introducing innovative ideas.

Whether the field was politics, agriculture, science or education, the period was alive with an air of inquiry and suggestions for the improvement of life in Iceland.

Dawn of Saltfish Exports

FOLLOWING THE OPENING by Danish merchants of fish curing and salting workshops, ships laden with a cargo of saltfish set sail for Spain.

Thus was introduced a lucrative trade link between the two countries, and saltfish exports to the Spanish market were to remain a crucial prop to Icelandic economic survival right up until the Second World War.

Although much reduced in importance for

modern-day Icelanders, the saltfish industry
is still very much alive in Iceland; indeed,
one of the world's largest sales organizations
for this marine delicacy is Icelandic.

1783 New Calamities

IN THE WAKE OF A SERIES of poor harvests
and eruptions, Icelanders were once more re-
minded of just how close they lived to the
capricious powers of nature.
In early 1783, the huge volcanic rift Laki,
west of Vatnajökull glacier, began what

turned out to be a one-year-long eruption. Immense amounts of lava came streaming down the mountain sides to create eventually the largest-ever lava field to be formed in historical times from a single eruption.

The eruption also released clouds of lethal gas and noxious fumes that poisoned plant life and killed an estimated fifty percent of Iceland's livestock.

Famine and fresh outbreaks of disease once again stalked Iceland, and up to 10,000 people perished.

1786 Prelude to Urbanization

THE BEGINNINGS of Iceland's present-day capital can be traced back to the granting in 1786 of Reykjavík's municipal charter.

The charter, which promoted the tiny village of 167 souls to an authorized trading centre, was the spur to a process of slow but steady urbanization.

Another positive move at the time was the abolition in 1787 of the infamous Danish trade monopoly that had for so long shackled Icelandic economic endeavour.

To coincide with the easing of trade restric-

tions, five other villages around the country were also granted municipal charters.

 ## Political Centralization

ICELAND HAD ALWAYS maintained a loosely linked system of local centres of power and influence, but towards the end of the eighteenth century there was a concerted effort to centralize power in the emerging capital, Reykjavík.

Even the venerable Althing was abolished, as were the episcopal see and the school at

Hólar, thus leaving Iceland with no political assembly and only one bishop, and the grand total of one school.

A national court was instead established in Reykjavík to absorb the functions of the Althing, although this Viking Age parliamentary institution was to remain a potent symbol in the Icelandic psyche.

The Adventurer King

DURING THE MAYHEM and distresses of the Napoleonic wars (1800-1815), English merchants and the Danish authorities began jockeying for power in Iceland.

Backed by English traders, a Danish adventurer serving in the British Navy, Jörgen Jörgensen, placed the Governor under arrest. This was, however, only the beginning of what is one of the more bizarre twists in the rich tapestry of Icelandic history, for Jörgensen declared an end to Danish rule and gave himself the title of Protector of all Iceland.

Lacking official support from London, Jörgensen was eventually removed by the British and shipped back to England, his

reign as self-styled "king" of Iceland having
endured only from June 26 to August 22.

 ## Birth of Jón Sigurdsson

THE FOREMOST LEADER of Iceland's struggle
to regain sovereignty, Jón Sigurdsson, was
born at Hrafnseyri in Iceland's West Fjords
on June 17, 1811.

Tutored at home, Sigurdsson went on to
study literature, languages and history at the
University of Copenhagen, the city in which
he was to spend most of his life.

An active scholar and writer, he also found time to work tirelessly for Icelandic political rights and the betterment of social and economic conditions in his homeland.

Sigurdsson is today a revered national hero whose birthday, June 17, is celebrated as the National Day of Iceland.

 ## Restoration of the Althing

INSPIRED BY THE WINDS of nationalism and Romanticism stirring through early nineteenth-century Europe, Icelanders began agitating for their own advisory assembly in Iceland.

The Danish King finally relented, and in 1843 it was decided to restore the Althing, but this time it was to be situated in Reykjavík.

Two more years were to pass before the first meeting of the reconstituted assembly, made up of twenty elected members and six representatives appointed by the King.

1855 Free Trade

EVEN THOUGH THE TRADE monopoly had been lifted in 1787, the right to trade was strictly limited to subjects of the King of Denmark.

But now the last barrier to open and free trade in the country was removed.

This event marked the beginning of modern Icelandic society, as it provided the basis upon which Icelanders could at long last enjoy the benefits of the technical and industrial revolution sweeping the world.

Emigration

THE MID-NINETEENTH CENTURY saw the first tentative beginnings of emigration from Iceland when a group of Mormon converts left for Utah in 1855, to be followed five years later by a group bound for Brazil. Most emigration however, was to North America, particularly to the land west of Lake Winnipeg in Canada.

It is estimated that some ten percent of the population at that time made the arduous journey westward over the Atlantic.

The Constitution

IN 1874, 1,000 YEARS after Ingólfur Arnarson had first settled in Reykjavík, the Danish King, Christian IX, presented Iceland with a new constitution that in many respects is still in force.

The new document passed the power over legislative and financial matters to the Althing, but ultimate executive authority still rested with the King.

Along with the increase in Icelanders' control over their domestic affairs came consti-

tutional guarantees of a range of basic civil and
personal liberties, including the right of free
speech and religious tolerance.

 ## Askja Erupts

ONE OF THE MOST powerful volcanic eruptions
ever recorded was the outpouring from Askja
volcano north of Vatnajökull glacier. The
eruption began at Easter time and apart from
destroying huge tracts of land soon produced
an immense volume of ash that thickly blan-
keted the entire eastern region of Iceland.

It was not long before clouds of ash spread across the northern hemisphere, reaching, among other places, Sweden and Russia. A by-product of the eruption was a huge water-filled depression, Öskjuvatn lake, that is Iceland's deepest with a depth of 217 metres.

Mechanized Industry

THE EARLIEST YEARS of the twentieth century were revolutionary as far as the development of Iceland's fisheries and transport are concerned.

Shipped to the country in fishing vessels powered by tiny diesel engines, the fruit of the industrial revolution soon had a sweeping impact on Icelandic society.

There was a dramatic rise in the number of trawlers acquired by the Icelanders, and the country's first motor car made its appearance in 1904.

Home Rule

A MAJOR SHIFT towards liberalism in Denmark in 1901 sowed the seeds for a radical

political breakthrough three years later in
Iceland.

In 1904 the unthinkable finally occurred,
and Hannes Hafstein, an Icelander, was appointed as Minister for Iceland by the King
of Denmark. Just as important, the new minister was based in Reykjavík and not in distant Copenhagen.

Although Iceland was still an integral part of
the Kingdom of Denmark, the move to
home rule was a significant event that
brought the base of real decision making
back to Icelandic soil.

1906 Linked to the World

THE LAYING OF ICELAND'S first telegraph cable, from Scotland via the Faroes to Seydisfjördur on the east coast and then on to Reykjavík, was completed in 1906. With the cable, Icelanders could at long last begin to emerge from the murk of isolation that had descended upon their nation with the loss of independence and the waning of its medieval glory days. Telecommunications improved rapidly, and in 1935, international telephone links were established.

1910 First Daily Newspaper

THE EARLY DECADES of this century saw rapid progress. Hot on the heels of the introduction of the telegraph came the founding of the country's first regular daily newspaper, although periodicals and other publications had been printed since 1848.

Iceland's first newspaper was called *Vísir*, and after its merger with *Dagbladid* can now be bought under the name *DV* at news agents' kiosks all over the country. The largest daily in Iceland is *Morgunbladid*, founded in 1913.

 # The University of Iceland

ICELAND'S PROUD TRADITION of higher
learning, centred around Episcopal schools
dating from the Middle Ages, went into de-
cline under the centuries of colonial rule.
Following extensive planning at the beginning of the century, Icelanders finally established their own institution, the University of
Iceland, for which the old training colleges
for medicine, theology and law were combined with a new department for Icelandic

studies. The University of Iceland today has nine faculties serving over 5,000 students.

The Icelandic Flag

THE MODERN ICELANDIC national flag of red, white and blue was approved for use by the King of Denmark at a time when most Icelanders really wanted to use a simple white cross on a blue background.

The King thought that the blue and white design was too similar to the Greek flag, and he refused to give his consent, despite it being the flag of choice of parliament.

Instead, the King gave the go-ahead to the use of the alternate second choice design that still flutters above the Althing.

Sovereignty

AS EUROPE'S AGE of empire, shattered by the carnage of World War I, gave way to the age of democracy, the stage was set for Iceland to regain her sovereignty.

A treaty, passed by the Danish and Icelandic parliaments and a referendum in Iceland, made Iceland a free and independent country

under the same King as Denmark, with the
right to full independence after twenty-five
years.
On December 1, 1918, one of the most
memorable days in Iceland's history, the
Danish flag was lowered from across Iceland
to be replaced by a red and white cross on an
ultramarine background.

 First Woman Parliamentarian

AT LAST THE FIRST WOMAN, Ingibjörg H.
Bjarnason, was elected to Iceland's parlia-

ment – the result of a long campaign for women's rights.

Women received the right to vote in local elections in 1907, the same year that the Federation for Women's Rights was formed. It was not until 1915 however that the franchise for parliamentary elections was extended to women, and then only at age forty, as compared to twenty-five for men. Universal and equal suffrage was eventually introduced in 1920.

 Radio Days

ICELAND'S STATE-OPERATED radio service began broadcasting in 1930, offering the then conventional fare of culture and entertainment.

The fledgling service was defiantly neutral in politics, a trait that fortunately has been maintained to the present day.

The service's second channel, Rás 2, came on air in 1983 and continues to provide mostly popular music and light entertainment.

Following the removal of the state monopoly of the airwaves in 1986, a rash of new

independent stations began offering an even wider range of programming for people of all ages.

The Great Depression

AS WAS THE CASE with many countries across the world, much of the nineteen-thirties in Iceland was a time of economic collapse and grinding hardship.

Almost entirely dependent on the export of unprocessed goods, mainly fish, Iceland had no advanced economic structure to cushion the blows of the depression; exacerbating the situation was the fact that Iceland's main export market, Spain, was embroiled in the agonies of civil war from 1936-1939.

It was only with the coming of the Second World War that the economic gloom began to lift.

1934 Social Insurance

LEGISLATION IN THE MID-THIRTIES sowed the seeds of Iceland's advanced social welfare and health care systems.

By introducing an insurance scheme, even the most disadvantaged sections of society were guaranteed a minimum level of assistance and support from public funds.

Together with the beginnings of this "womb to tomb" system of social programmes, the government also launched a series of concerted efforts to tackle the unemployment crisis.

1937 Icelandair Takes Off

THE FIRST FLIGHTS in Iceland were made in 1919, and five years later the first aeroplane from Europe landed in the country.

One of the forerunners of Icelandair was established, following numerous experiments, in 1937, and initially offered scheduled flights between Akureyri in the north and Reykjavík.
The company began international services in 1946, as did another airline, Loftleidir, one year later.
Both airlines merged in 1973 to form present-day Icelandair, which operates a comprehensive network of domestic and international routes.

Arrival of British Forces

ON MAY 10, the same day that Germany ended the "Phony War" and launched the Blitzkrieg on Western Europe, British forces landed in Reykjavík to pre-empt a feared German takeover of the country. Although the British maintained a presence until 1945, it was the Americans, who arrived in the summer of 1941, who took over the bulk of Iceland's defences. The arrival of foreign military forces sparked a massive economic boom in Iceland, as offices, airfields and installations had to be constructed for the thousands of Allied troops that poured into the country.

 # Declaration of the Republic of Iceland

PARLIAMENT VOTED to revoke the 1918 Union treaty with Denmark, and a referendum with a 98% turnout was overwhelmingly in favour, with 95% wishing to break all remaining links with the Danish Crown. The way was clear for Iceland to become a fully independent country, and on June 17, the birthday of Jón Sigurdsson, leader of the national-

ist movement in the 19th century, the Republic of Iceland was proclaimed at Thingvellir, site of the country's ancient parliament or Althing. The first president of the Icelandic Republic was Sveinn Björnsson, chosen by parliament in 1944 and returned in an election in 1948.

1946 1949 Iceland and the International Community

BECAUSE ICELAND was opposed to declaring war on any nation, the country could not meet the demands of the Allied powers on becoming a founding member of the United Nations in 1945. Despite this initial obstacle, Iceland became a member of the UN in 1946, and remains a committed and active participant in the organization. The outbreak of the Cold War and the lack of any defences on Icelandic soil led to Iceland joining the North Atlantic Treaty Organization (NATO) as a founding member in 1949.

1950 A National Theatre and Orchestra

THERE HAD BEEN THEATRE in Reykjavík since 1897, but it was not until the building of the National Theatre in 1950 that a professional theatre company and a symphony orchestra were founded – in spite of the fact that Reykjavík's population was a mere 70,000 at the time. The public's appetite for theatrical productions has grown and the capital now boasts two large professional companies, a range of amateur groups, opera and ballet. In addition to the orchestra, there are a number of smaller ensembles catering to classical music audiences, not to mention a very large number of choirs.

1952 Extension of Fisheries Limits

FOREIGN VESSELS had been working the rich fishing grounds off Iceland's coast for hundreds of years, but since the beginning of the twentieth century, Iceland had a fisheries limit of three miles.

With the extension of the country's exclusive fisheries zone to four miles in 1952, all fjords and inlets were closed to trawlers, and measures were introduced to prevent overfishing. The British protested strongly, fish from Iceland was boycotted and Icelandic ships were banned from landing their catches in UK ports. But new markets were found and eventually the British lifted the ban.

 ## 1955 Halldór Laxness Receives Nobel Prize for Literature

HALLDÓR LAXNESS is to date the only Icelander to have been awarded the Nobel Prize for Literature – which is still no mean feat considering the country's tiny population. Laxness dealt with a vast range of subjects in his work, much of which has been translated into the world's leading languages.

He was also a controversial writer, principally because of his outspoken views on politics, religion and the environment.

Following his Nobel achievement however, there was a reconciliation between the grand old man of modern Icelandic letters and his countrymen.

 ## 1963 The Fiery Birth of Surtsey Island

EARLY ON THE MORNING of November 14, 1963, steam was seen billowing above the

sea southwest off the Westman Islands off Iceland's southern coast.
The following day a new island had arisen from beneath the waves, the result of powerful submarine volcanic activity. The eruption lasted until June 1967, the end result being a 2.7km² island that was named Surtsey, or Isle of Surtur, the fire giant of Norse mythology. A natural protection zone, Surtsey has offered scientists a unique opportunity to research the beginnings of plant life in practically untouched surroundings.

1966 Beginning of Television Broadcasts

THE STATE BROADCASTING Service began TV
transmissions on a twice-weekly basis in 1966.
The service gradually expanded, although in
order to give people some respite, Thursdays
were TV-free until 1986.

Along with the introduction of programming
on Thursdays came the lifting of the state monopoly on broadcasting, so that today there are
a number of stations available in Iceland, the
two largest being the state-run service and the
commercial Channel Two.

1968 The Nordic House

ICELAND HAS BEEN a member of the five-na-
tion Nordic Council since 1952, and has
played an active role in this body which has
done so much to strengthen links between the
Nordic countries.

In 1968 a Nordic cultural centre, the Nordic
House, was opened close to the city centre in
Reykjavík; the building was specially designed
by the renowned Finnish architect Alvar
Aalto.

There are conference rooms, an exhibition gallery and a library located in the centre where various activities take place all year round, and visitors from the other Nordic countries frequent the centre, both as performers and guests.

Return of the Manuscripts

A LARGE NUMBER of Icelandic manuscripts had been sent by scholars to Denmark in the 17th and 18th centuries, and one of the most famous collectors had been the Icelander Árni Magnússon, who was based in Copenhagen.

With the coming of full independence, Iceland began a campaign for the return of these manuscripts, claiming they were national treasures. Despite the opposition of many Danish experts and politicians it was agreed that they should be returned.

Such an example of the repatriation of artistic treasures remains an extremely rare occurrence.

1973 The Heimaey Eruption

ON THE NIGHT OF JANUARY 23, 1973, the 5,300 souls of Heimaey, a crucial fishing centre in the Westman Islands off the south coast of Iceland, were roused from their sleep by an immense volcanic eruption right on their doorsteps.

Almost all the inhabitants were quickly rushed to safety in a fleet of fishing boats and no one got hurt.

The eruption continued for six months and caused widespread damage, but that did not stop the populace from returning to rebuild their beloved town.

1974 Female Clergy

AUDUR EIR VILHJÁLMSDÓTTIR became the first woman to be ordained a priest in Iceland's Lutheran Church, of which over 90% of the population are nominally members.

Women had been graduating with theology degrees from the University of Iceland for over thirty years, but none had yet been ordained. Female clergy have been generally well received in Iceland, and the vast majority of women theology graduates now become priests.

The Great 200-Mile Cod War

JURISDICTION OVER ITS marine resources is
vital to the economic survival of the Icelandic people, and in order to safeguard fishing stocks and to deter overfishing, Iceland
extended its fisheries limit to 4 miles in 1952.
This was followed by extensions to 12 miles
in 1958, to 50 miles in 1972 and finally to
200 miles in 1975.

Britain reacted by sending Royal Navy vessels
into Icelandic waters and setting landing
bans on Icelandic fishing boats, as well as try-
ing by other means to thwart the extension of
limits. The British authorities, however, have
always had to accede to Icelandic wishes in
this area.

 # A Woman President

VIGDÍS FINNBOGADÓTTIR, the fourth president of the Icelandic republic, was the first
woman to be elected head-of-state in a parliamentary democracy.

Another landmark was the mass strike by Iceland's women on October 24, 1975, for a
greater role in society. What made this partic-

ular instance of industrial action special was
that the strike affected not only workplaces
but also Icelandic homes.

The election of President Finnbogadóttir
was the result of a long campaign for greater
women's rights in Iceland, a campaign that
also prompted the emergence of a female-
only slate for local and general elections that
has notched up some success at the polls.

 ## An End to Whaling

FOLLOWING THE 1980 decision by the In-

ternational Whaling Commission to ban
whaling in the northern seas by 1986,
Iceland ceased commercial whaling.

The taking of small amounts of whales
for scientific purposes continued until
1989, when this too was discontinued by
Iceland.

Both domestic and international research had established that the species
of whale formerly harvested by Icelanders was in absolutely no danger of
extinction.

 ## 1989 Toasting
the End of the Beer Ban

THE US WAS NOT the only nation ide-
alistic enough to impose prohibition
upon itself – Iceland too had its ban on
the production and consumption of alcohol.

The alcohol drought lasted from 1915 to
1935, but the sale of light wines was al-
lowed in 1922, as part of an effort to
boost the saltfish trade with Spain.

A ban on strong beer was kept in force
however after 1935, and it was not until

March 1, 1989 that a grateful nation could legally slake its thirst with the frothy brew.

 ## The National Library

IT IS FITTING THAT the opening of Iceland's new National Library Centre should have coincided with the 50th anniversary of the declaration of the Republic of Iceland. The library combines the extensive collections of the University Library and the old National Library, both of which had been housed in cramped inadequate buildings.

The new home for the National Library is a daring user-friendly structure a few minutes' stroll from the University campus.

Epilogue

When one looks over the route of Icelandic history and lingers at some of its milestones, it is a pleasant surprise to see how peaceful, when compared to other nations, Iceland's development has been.

War and strife occurred seldom and belong to the events of distant centuries, although Icelanders have paid dearly for their dependence on the forces of nature.

Despite this, Icelanders have always lived in harmony with their surroundings, and have constantly striven to utilise nature's resources in a sensible manner.

This close bond with nature is evident in many aspects of Icelandic life and has moulded the evolution of society on this island.

Another striking feature of Icelandic life is the distinctive way in which Iceland's language and culture have matured over 1,000 years.

The Icelanders are aware of their roots, and in the Middle Ages they wrote a literature that defies comparison with anything the rest of Europe has to offer from the period.

The natural background and the legacy of the sagas are the true guiding spirits of Icelandic national life, no matter how much Icelanders have taken to modern gadgetry and international trends.

Icelanders today number some 270,000 and live with one of the world's highest standards of living when measured by the yardstick of consumption. One thing seems clear however, the Icelandic nation would never have come this far without being firmly rooted in the soil and heritage of Iceland.